50 Banana Recipes for Home

By: Kelly Johnson

Table of Contents

- Classic Banana Bread
- Banana Muffins
- Banana Pancakes
- Banana Waffles
- Banana Smoothie
- Banana Oatmeal Cookies
- Banana Cream Pie
- Banana Fritters
- Banana Nut Bread
- Banana Pudding
- Banana Chocolate Chip Muffins
- Banana French Toast
- Banana Nutella Crepes
- Banana Oat Bars
- Banana Chia Seed Pudding
- Banana Nut Smoothie
- Banana Coconut Cake
- Banana Ice Cream
- Banana Foster
- Banana Nutella Smoothie
- Banana Cheesecake
- Banana Cinnamon Rolls
- Banana Bread Pudding
- Banana Coconut Muffins
- Banana and Peanut Butter Smoothie
- Banana and Strawberry Smoothie
- Banana Split
- Banana Walnut Muffins
- Banana Almond Smoothie
- Banana Pecan Pie
- Banana Cinnamon Oatmeal
- Banana Oat Pancakes
- Banana and Date Energy Balls
- Banana Cream Bars

- Banana Chocolate Chip Cookies
- Banana Coconut Energy Balls
- Banana Raisin Bread
- Banana Peanut Butter Bars
- Banana Caramel Cake
- Banana and Yogurt Parfait
- Banana Maple Muffins
- Banana Crumb Cake
- Banana Chocolate Smoothie
- Banana Berry Smoothie
- Banana Almond Cake
- Banana Nut Cupcakes
- Banana Pineapple Smoothie
- Banana and Nut Granola
- Banana Cheesecake Bars
- Banana Pudding Trifle

Classic Banana Bread

Ingredients:

- 1 ½ cups all-purpose flour
- 1 tsp baking powder
- ½ tsp baking soda
- ¼ tsp salt
- ½ cup unsalted butter, softened
- ¾ cup granulated sugar
- 2 large eggs
- 1 cup mashed ripe bananas (about 3 bananas)
- 1 tsp vanilla extract

Instructions:

1. **Prepare the Oven and Pan:**
   1. Preheat your oven to 350°F (175°C). Grease and flour a 9x5-inch loaf pan.
2. **Mix Dry Ingredients:**
   1. In a bowl, whisk together flour, baking powder, baking soda, and salt.
3. **Cream Butter and Sugar:**
   1. In a large bowl, cream together butter and sugar until light and fluffy.
   2. Beat in eggs one at a time, then mix in mashed bananas and vanilla extract.
4. **Combine and Bake:**
   1. Gradually add the dry ingredients to the wet ingredients, mixing until just combined.
   2. Pour batter into the prepared loaf pan.
   3. Bake for 60-70 minutes, or until a toothpick inserted into the center comes out clean.
5. **Cool and Serve:**
   1. Allow to cool in the pan for 10 minutes, then transfer to a wire rack to cool completely.

Banana Muffins

Ingredients:

- 1 ½ cups all-purpose flour
- 1 tsp baking powder
- ½ tsp baking soda
- ¼ tsp salt
- ½ cup unsalted butter, softened
- ¾ cup granulated sugar
- 2 large eggs
- 1 cup mashed ripe bananas (about 3 bananas)
- 1 tsp vanilla extract

Instructions:

1. **Prepare the Oven and Pan:**
    1. Preheat your oven to 350°F (175°C). Line a muffin tin with paper liners.
2. **Mix Dry Ingredients:**
    1. In a bowl, whisk together flour, baking powder, baking soda, and salt.
3. **Cream Butter and Sugar:**
    1. In a large bowl, cream together butter and sugar until light and fluffy.
    2. Beat in eggs one at a time, then mix in mashed bananas and vanilla extract.
4. **Combine and Bake:**
    1. Gradually add the dry ingredients to the wet ingredients, mixing until just combined.
    2. Divide batter evenly among muffin cups.
    3. Bake for 18-22 minutes, or until a toothpick inserted into the center comes out clean.
5. **Cool and Serve:**
    1. Allow muffins to cool in the tin for 5 minutes, then transfer to a wire rack to cool completely.

Banana Pancakes

Ingredients:

- 1 cup all-purpose flour
- 2 tbsp sugar
- 2 tsp baking powder
- ¼ tsp salt
- 1 cup milk
- 1 large egg
- 2 tbsp unsalted butter, melted
- 1 cup mashed ripe bananas (about 2 bananas)

Instructions:

1. **Mix Dry Ingredients:**
    1. In a bowl, whisk together flour, sugar, baking powder, and salt.
2. **Combine Wet Ingredients:**
    1. In another bowl, whisk together milk, egg, and melted butter.
    2. Stir in mashed bananas.
3. **Combine and Cook:**
    1. Gradually add the wet ingredients to the dry ingredients, mixing until just combined.
    2. Heat a griddle or skillet over medium heat and lightly grease.
    3. Pour ¼ cup of batter onto the griddle for each pancake. Cook until bubbles form on the surface, then flip and cook until golden brown.
4. **Serve:**
    1. Serve warm with your favorite toppings.

Banana Waffles

Ingredients:

- 1 ½ cups all-purpose flour
- 2 tbsp sugar
- 1 tbsp baking powder
- ¼ tsp salt
- 1 cup milk
- 2 large eggs
- ½ cup unsalted butter, melted
- 1 cup mashed ripe bananas (about 2 bananas)
- 1 tsp vanilla extract

Instructions:

1. **Prepare the Waffle Iron:**
    1. Preheat your waffle iron according to the manufacturer's instructions.
2. **Mix Dry Ingredients:**
    1. In a bowl, whisk together flour, sugar, baking powder, and salt.
3. **Combine Wet Ingredients:**
    1. In another bowl, whisk together milk, eggs, melted butter, mashed bananas, and vanilla extract.
4. **Combine and Cook:**
    1. Gradually add the wet ingredients to the dry ingredients, mixing until just combined.
    2. Pour batter onto the preheated waffle iron and cook according to the manufacturer's instructions.
5. **Serve:**
    1. Serve warm with your favorite toppings.

Banana Smoothie

Ingredients:

- 1 ripe banana
- 1 cup milk (or a dairy-free alternative)
- ½ cup plain or vanilla yogurt
- 1 tbsp honey or maple syrup (optional)
- 1 cup ice

Instructions:

1. **Blend Ingredients:**
    1. In a blender, combine banana, milk, yogurt, honey (if using), and ice.
    2. Blend until smooth.
2. **Serve:**
    1. Pour into glasses and serve immediately.

Banana Oatmeal Cookies

Ingredients:

- 1 cup rolled oats
- 1 cup mashed ripe bananas (about 2 bananas)
- ¼ cup brown sugar
- ½ tsp cinnamon
- ¼ cup chocolate chips (optional)

Instructions:

1. **Preheat the Oven:**
    1. Preheat your oven to 350°F (175°C) and line a baking sheet with parchment paper.
2. **Mix Ingredients:**
    1. In a bowl, combine oats, mashed bananas, brown sugar, and cinnamon.
    2. Stir in chocolate chips if using.
3. **Form Cookies:**
    1. Drop spoonfuls of dough onto the prepared baking sheet.
4. **Bake:**
    1. Bake for 10-12 minutes, or until edges are golden brown.
5. **Cool and Serve:**
    1. Allow cookies to cool on the baking sheet for a few minutes before transferring to a wire rack to cool completely.

Banana Cream Pie

Ingredients:

- **For the Crust:**
    - 1 ½ cups graham cracker crumbs
    - ¼ cup granulated sugar
    - 6 tbsp unsalted butter, melted
- **For the Filling:**
    - 1 cup whole milk
    - ½ cup granulated sugar
    - ¼ cup cornstarch
    - ¼ tsp salt
    - 3 large egg yolks
    - 2 tbsp unsalted butter
    - 1 tsp vanilla extract
    - 2 ripe bananas, sliced
- **For the Whipped Cream Topping:**
    - 1 cup heavy cream
    - 2 tbsp powdered sugar
    - 1 tsp vanilla extract

Instructions:

1. **Prepare the Crust:**
    1. Preheat your oven to 350°F (175°C).
    2. In a bowl, combine graham cracker crumbs, sugar, and melted butter. Press mixture into the bottom and sides of a 9-inch pie dish.
    3. Bake for 8-10 minutes, then allow to cool.
2. **Prepare the Filling:**
    1. In a medium saucepan, whisk together milk, sugar, cornstarch, and salt. Cook over medium heat, stirring constantly, until mixture thickens.
    2. In a bowl, whisk egg yolks, then gradually add a small amount of the hot mixture to temper the eggs. Stir the egg mixture back into the saucepan.
    3. Continue cooking for 1-2 minutes, then remove from heat and stir in butter and vanilla extract.
    4. Allow to cool slightly, then fold in sliced bananas.
3. **Assemble and Chill:**

1. Pour filling into the cooled crust and smooth the top.
2. Refrigerate for at least 4 hours or until set.
4. **Prepare the Whipped Cream:**
    1. In a bowl, whip heavy cream, powdered sugar, and vanilla extract until stiff peaks form.
    2. Spread whipped cream over the chilled pie.
5. **Serve:**
    1. Slice and serve chilled.

Banana Fritters

Ingredients:

- 3 ripe bananas, mashed
- 1 cup all-purpose flour
- 2 tbsp granulated sugar
- 1 tsp baking powder
- ¼ tsp salt
- 1 large egg
- ¼ cup milk
- Vegetable oil for frying
- Powdered sugar for dusting

Instructions:

1. **Prepare the Batter:**
    1. In a bowl, combine flour, sugar, baking powder, and salt.
    2. In another bowl, mix mashed bananas, egg, and milk.
    3. Gradually add the dry ingredients to the wet ingredients, mixing until just combined.
2. **Fry the Fritters:**
    1. Heat oil in a skillet over medium heat.
    2. Drop spoonfuls of batter into the hot oil and cook until golden brown, about 2-3 minutes per side.
    3. Remove fritters with a slotted spoon and drain on paper towels.
3. **Serve:**
    1. Dust with powdered sugar before serving.

Banana Nut Bread

Ingredients:

- 1 ½ cups all-purpose flour
- 1 tsp baking powder
- ½ tsp baking soda
- ¼ tsp salt
- ½ cup unsalted butter, softened
- ¾ cup granulated sugar
- 2 large eggs
- 1 cup mashed ripe bananas (about 3 bananas)
- 1 tsp vanilla extract
- ½ cup chopped walnuts

Instructions:

1. **Prepare the Oven and Pan:**
    1. Preheat your oven to 350°F (175°C). Grease and flour a 9x5-inch loaf pan.
2. **Mix Dry Ingredients:**
    1. In a bowl, whisk together flour, baking powder, baking soda, and salt.
3. **Cream Butter and Sugar:**
    1. In a large bowl, cream together butter and sugar until light and fluffy.
    2. Beat in eggs one at a time, then mix in mashed bananas and vanilla extract.
4. **Combine and Bake:**
    1. Gradually add the dry ingredients to the wet ingredients, mixing until just combined.
    2. Fold in chopped walnuts.
    3. Pour batter into the prepared loaf pan.
    4. Bake for 60-70 minutes, or until a toothpick inserted into the center comes out clean.
5. **Cool and Serve:**
    1. Allow to cool in the pan for 10 minutes, then transfer to a wire rack to cool completely.

Banana Pudding

Ingredients:

- 1 cup whole milk
- ½ cup granulated sugar
- ¼ cup cornstarch
- ¼ tsp salt
- 3 large egg yolks
- 2 tbsp unsalted butter
- 1 tsp vanilla extract
- 3 ripe bananas, sliced
- 1 cup whipped cream or whipped topping
- Vanilla wafer cookies

Instructions:

1. **Prepare the Pudding:**
    1. In a medium saucepan, whisk together milk, sugar, cornstarch, and salt.
    2. Cook over medium heat, stirring constantly, until the mixture thickens.
    3. In a bowl, whisk egg yolks, then gradually add a small amount of the hot mixture to temper the eggs. Stir the egg mixture back into the saucepan.
    4. Continue cooking for 1-2 minutes, then remove from heat and stir in butter and vanilla extract.
2. **Assemble the Pudding:**
    1. In a serving dish, layer vanilla wafer cookies, sliced bananas, and pudding.
    2. Repeat layers, ending with pudding.
3. **Top and Chill:**
    1. Spread whipped cream over the top.
    2. Refrigerate for at least 4 hours or until set.
4. **Serve:**
    1. Serve chilled.

Banana Chocolate Chip Muffins

Ingredients:

- 1 ½ cups all-purpose flour
- ½ tsp baking powder
- ½ tsp baking soda
- ¼ tsp salt
- ½ cup unsalted butter, softened
- ¾ cup granulated sugar
- 2 large eggs
- 1 cup mashed ripe bananas (about 3 bananas)
- ½ cup mini chocolate chips
- 1 tsp vanilla extract

Instructions:

1. **Prepare the Oven and Pan:**
    1. Preheat your oven to 350°F (175°C). Line a muffin tin with paper liners.
2. **Mix Dry Ingredients:**
    1. In a bowl, whisk together flour, baking powder, baking soda, and salt.
3. **Cream Butter and Sugar:**
    1. In a large bowl, cream together butter and sugar until light and fluffy.
    2. Beat in eggs one at a time, then mix in mashed bananas and vanilla extract.
4. **Combine and Bake:**
    1. Gradually add the dry ingredients to the wet ingredients, mixing until just combined.
    2. Fold in chocolate chips.
    3. Divide batter evenly among muffin cups.
    4. Bake for 18-22 minutes, or until a toothpick inserted into the center comes out clean.
5. **Cool and Serve:**
    1. Allow muffins to cool in the tin for 5 minutes, then transfer to a wire rack to cool completely.

Banana French Toast

Ingredients:

- 2 ripe bananas, mashed
- 4 large eggs
- 1 cup milk
- 1 tsp vanilla extract
- ¼ tsp ground cinnamon
- 8 slices bread (preferably stale)
- 2 tbsp unsalted butter
- Maple syrup for serving

Instructions:

1. **Prepare the Batter:**
    1. In a bowl, whisk together mashed bananas, eggs, milk, vanilla extract, and cinnamon.
2. **Cook the French Toast:**
    1. Heat butter in a skillet over medium heat.
    2. Dip each slice of bread into the banana mixture, allowing excess to drip off.
    3. Cook bread slices in the skillet until golden brown, about 2-3 minutes per side.
3. **Serve:**
    1. Serve warm with maple syrup.

Banana Nutella Crepes

Ingredients:

- **For the Crepes:**
    - 1 cup all-purpose flour
    - 2 large eggs
    - 1 cup milk
    - 2 tbsp unsalted butter, melted
    - 1 tbsp granulated sugar
    - ¼ tsp salt
- **For the Filling:**
    - ½ cup Nutella
    - 2 ripe bananas, sliced

Instructions:

1. **Prepare the Crepe Batter:**
    1. In a bowl, whisk together flour, eggs, milk, melted butter, sugar, and salt until smooth.
2. **Cook the Crepes:**
    1. Heat a non-stick skillet over medium heat and lightly grease.
    2. Pour ¼ cup of batter into the skillet and swirl to spread evenly.
    3. Cook until the edges start to lift and bubbles form, then flip and cook the other side.
3. **Assemble and Serve:**
    1. Spread Nutella over each crepe, then top with banana slices.
    2. Fold or roll crepes and serve immediately.

Banana Chia Seed Pudding

Ingredients:

- 1 cup milk (dairy or non-dairy)
- ¼ cup chia seeds
- 2 tbsp maple syrup or honey
- 1 tsp vanilla extract
- 1 ripe banana, mashed
- Fresh fruit for topping (optional)

Instructions:

1. **Combine Ingredients:**
    1. In a bowl, mix together milk, chia seeds, maple syrup (or honey), and vanilla extract.
    2. Stir in mashed banana.
2. **Chill:**
    1. Cover and refrigerate for at least 4 hours or overnight, stirring occasionally.
3. **Serve:**
    1. Top with fresh fruit if desired and serve chilled.

Banana Nut Smoothie

Ingredients:

- 1 ripe banana
- 1 cup milk (dairy or non-dairy)
- ¼ cup Greek yogurt
- 2 tbsp almond butter or peanut butter
- 1 tbsp honey or maple syrup
- ¼ cup chopped nuts (such as almonds or walnuts)
- 1 cup ice

Instructions:

1. **Blend Ingredients:**
    1. In a blender, combine banana, milk, Greek yogurt, almond butter, honey, and ice.
    2. Blend until smooth.
2. **Serve:**
    1. Pour into glasses and sprinkle with chopped nuts.

Banana Coconut Cake

Ingredients:

- **For the Cake:**
    - 1 ½ cups all-purpose flour
    - 1 cup granulated sugar
    - 1 tsp baking powder
    - ½ tsp baking soda
    - ¼ tsp salt
    - ½ cup unsalted butter, softened
    - 2 large eggs
    - 1 cup mashed ripe bananas (about 3 bananas)
    - ½ cup shredded coconut
    - 1 tsp vanilla extract
- **For the Frosting:**
    - ½ cup unsalted butter, softened
    - 2 cups powdered sugar
    - 2 tbsp milk
    - 1 tsp vanilla extract
    - ¼ cup shredded coconut

Instructions:

1. **Prepare the Oven and Pan:**
    1. Preheat your oven to 350°F (175°C). Grease and flour a 9-inch round cake pan.
2. **Mix Dry Ingredients:**
    1. In a bowl, whisk together flour, sugar, baking powder, baking soda, and salt.
3. **Cream Butter and Sugar:**
    1. In a large bowl, cream together butter and sugar until light and fluffy.
    2. Beat in eggs one at a time, then mix in mashed bananas, shredded coconut, and vanilla extract.
4. **Combine and Bake:**
    1. Gradually add the dry ingredients to the wet ingredients, mixing until just combined.
    2. Pour batter into the prepared pan.

3. Bake for 30-35 minutes, or until a toothpick inserted into the center comes out clean.

5. **Prepare the Frosting:**
    1. In a bowl, beat together butter, powdered sugar, milk, and vanilla extract until smooth.
6. **Assemble and Frost:**
    1. Allow the cake to cool completely before frosting.
    2. Spread frosting over the cooled cake and sprinkle with additional shredded coconut.
7. **Serve:**
    1. Slice and serve.

Banana Ice Cream

Ingredients:

- 4 ripe bananas
- 1 tsp vanilla extract
- Optional mix-ins: chocolate chips, nuts, berries

Instructions:

1. **Prepare the Bananas:**
    1. Peel and slice bananas. Freeze slices until solid, about 2 hours.
2. **Blend:**
    1. In a food processor or blender, blend frozen banana slices and vanilla extract until smooth.
    2. Add optional mix-ins if desired and pulse a few times to combine.
3. **Serve:**
    1. Serve immediately as soft-serve or freeze for an additional 1-2 hours for a firmer texture.

Banana Foster

Ingredients:

- 2 ripe bananas, sliced
- ¼ cup unsalted butter
- ½ cup brown sugar
- ¼ cup dark rum
- 1 tsp cinnamon
- Vanilla ice cream for serving

Instructions:

1. **Prepare the Sauce:**
    1. In a skillet, melt butter over medium heat.
    2. Stir in brown sugar and cinnamon until dissolved and bubbly.
2. **Cook the Bananas:**
    1. Add banana slices to the skillet and cook for 1-2 minutes, until softened and coated in the sauce.
3. **Flambe (optional):**
    1. Carefully add rum to the skillet and ignite with a long lighter to flambé. Allow the flames to subside and the alcohol to burn off.
4. **Serve:**
    1. Serve over vanilla ice cream.

Banana Nutella Smoothie

Ingredients:

- 1 ripe banana
- 1 cup milk (dairy or non-dairy)
- 2 tbsp Nutella
- ¼ cup Greek yogurt
- 1 tbsp honey or maple syrup
- 1 cup ice

Instructions:

1. **Blend Ingredients:**
    1. In a blender, combine banana, milk, Nutella, Greek yogurt, honey, and ice.
    2. Blend until smooth.
2. **Serve:**
    1. Pour into glasses and serve immediately.

Banana Cheesecake

Ingredients:

- **For the Crust:**
    - 1 ½ cups graham cracker crumbs
    - ¼ cup granulated sugar
    - 6 tbsp unsalted butter, melted
- **For the Filling:**
    - 4 (8 oz) packages cream cheese, softened
    - 1 cup granulated sugar
    - 1 tsp vanilla extract
    - 3 large eggs
    - 1 cup mashed ripe bananas (about 2 bananas)
    - 1 cup sour cream
- **For the Topping (optional):**
    - Sliced bananas
    - Caramel sauce

Instructions:

1. **Prepare the Crust:**
    1. Preheat your oven to 325°F (160°C). Grease a 9-inch springform pan.
2. **Mix Crust Ingredients:**
    1. In a bowl, combine graham cracker crumbs, sugar, and melted butter.
    2. Press mixture into the bottom of the prepared pan.
3. **Prepare the Filling:**
    1. In a large bowl, beat cream cheese until smooth. Add sugar and vanilla extract, mixing until combined.
    2. Beat in eggs one at a time, then mix in mashed bananas and sour cream.
4. **Bake:**
    1. Pour filling into the crust.
    2. Bake for 50-60 minutes, or until the center is set and the edges are slightly golden.
5. **Cool and Serve:**
    1. Allow cheesecake to cool completely in the pan, then refrigerate for at least 4 hours or overnight.
    2. Top with sliced bananas and caramel sauce before serving if desired.

Banana Cinnamon Rolls

Ingredients:

- **For the Dough:**
    - 2 ¾ cups all-purpose flour
    - ¼ cup granulated sugar
    - 1 packet (2 ¼ tsp) active dry yeast
    - ½ tsp salt
    - ½ cup milk
    - ¼ cup water
    - ¼ cup unsalted butter, softened
    - 1 large egg
- **For the Filling:**
    - ¼ cup unsalted butter, softened
    - ½ cup brown sugar
    - 1 tbsp ground cinnamon
    - 1 cup mashed ripe bananas (about 2 bananas)
- **For the Glaze:**
    - 1 cup powdered sugar
    - 2 tbsp milk
    - ½ tsp vanilla extract

Instructions:

1. **Prepare the Dough:**
    1. In a large bowl, combine flour, sugar, yeast, and salt.
    2. In a saucepan, heat milk, water, and butter until warm and butter is melted.
    3. Add milk mixture to the flour mixture and stir until combined.
    4. Beat in the egg until dough forms.
    5. Knead dough on a floured surface for 5-7 minutes until smooth.
    6. Place dough in a greased bowl, cover, and let rise in a warm place for about 1 hour, or until doubled in size.
2. **Prepare the Filling:**
    1. In a bowl, mix together softened butter, brown sugar, cinnamon, and mashed bananas.
3. **Assemble and Bake:**
    1. Roll out dough on a floured surface into a rectangle.

2. Spread banana mixture evenly over dough.
   3. Roll up dough tightly and cut into 12 rolls.
   4. Place rolls in a greased baking dish and let rise for 30 minutes.
   5. Preheat oven to 350°F (175°C) and bake for 25-30 minutes, or until golden brown.
4. **Prepare the Glaze:**
   1. In a bowl, whisk together powdered sugar, milk, and vanilla extract until smooth.
   2. Drizzle over warm rolls.
5. **Serve:**
   1. Serve warm.

Banana Bread Pudding

Ingredients:

- 4 cups stale bread, cubed
- 2 cups milk
- ½ cup granulated sugar
- 4 large eggs
- 1 tsp vanilla extract
- 1 tsp ground cinnamon
- 1 cup mashed ripe bananas (about 2 bananas)
- ¼ cup melted butter
- ½ cup chopped nuts (optional)

Instructions:

1. **Prepare the Oven and Dish:**
    1. Preheat your oven to 350°F (175°C).
    2. Grease a 9x13-inch baking dish.
2. **Prepare the Mixture:**
    1. In a large bowl, whisk together milk, sugar, eggs, vanilla extract, and cinnamon.
    2. Stir in mashed bananas and melted butter.
    3. Add cubed bread and stir until evenly coated.
3. **Bake:**
    1. Pour mixture into the prepared baking dish.
    2. Sprinkle with chopped nuts if desired.
    3. Bake for 45-50 minutes, or until set and golden brown.
4. **Serve:**
    1. Serve warm with a scoop of vanilla ice cream or a drizzle of caramel sauce.

Banana Coconut Muffins

Ingredients:

- 1 ½ cups all-purpose flour
- ½ cup granulated sugar
- 1 tsp baking powder
- ½ tsp baking soda
- ¼ tsp salt
- ½ cup unsalted butter, melted
- 1 cup mashed ripe bananas (about 2 bananas)
- 1 cup shredded coconut
- 2 large eggs
- 1 tsp vanilla extract

Instructions:

1. **Prepare the Oven and Pan:**
    1. Preheat your oven to 350°F (175°C). Line a muffin tin with paper liners.
2. **Mix Dry Ingredients:**
    1. In a bowl, whisk together flour, sugar, baking powder, baking soda, and salt.
3. **Combine Wet Ingredients:**
    1. In another bowl, mix melted butter, mashed bananas, shredded coconut, eggs, and vanilla extract.
4. **Combine and Bake:**
    1. Gradually add the dry ingredients to the wet ingredients, mixing until just combined.
    2. Divide batter evenly among muffin cups.
    3. Bake for 18-22 minutes, or until a toothpick inserted into the center comes out clean.
5. **Cool and Serve:**
    1. Allow muffins to cool in the tin for 5 minutes, then transfer to a wire rack to cool completely.

Banana and Peanut Butter Smoothie

Ingredients:

- 1 ripe banana
- 1 cup milk (dairy or non-dairy)
- 2 tbsp peanut butter
- ½ cup Greek yogurt
- 1 tbsp honey or maple syrup
- 1 cup ice

Instructions:

1. **Blend Ingredients:**
    1. In a blender, combine banana, milk, peanut butter, Greek yogurt, honey, and ice.
    2. Blend until smooth.
2. **Serve:**
    1. Pour into glasses and serve immediately.

Banana and Strawberry Smoothie

Ingredients:

- 1 ripe banana
- 1 cup strawberries, fresh or frozen
- 1 cup milk (dairy or non-dairy)
- ½ cup Greek yogurt
- 1 tbsp honey or maple syrup
- 1 cup ice

Instructions:

1. **Blend Ingredients:**
    1. In a blender, combine banana, strawberries, milk, Greek yogurt, honey, and ice.
    2. Blend until smooth.
2. **Serve:**
    1. Pour into glasses and serve immediately.

Banana Split

Ingredients:

- 1 ripe banana
- 3 scoops vanilla ice cream
- ¼ cup chocolate syrup
- ¼ cup strawberry sauce
- ¼ cup crushed pineapple
- Whipped cream
- Maraschino cherries

Instructions:

1. **Prepare the Banana:**
    1. Slice the banana lengthwise and place in a serving dish.
2. **Assemble the Split:**
    1. Place scoops of vanilla ice cream between the banana slices.
    2. Drizzle with chocolate syrup, strawberry sauce, and crushed pineapple.
3. **Top and Serve:**
    1. Top with whipped cream and maraschino cherries.
    2. Serve immediately.

Banana Walnut Muffins

Ingredients:

- 1 ½ cups all-purpose flour
- ½ tsp baking powder
- ½ tsp baking soda
- ¼ tsp salt
- ½ cup unsalted butter, softened
- ¾ cup granulated sugar
- 2 large eggs
- 1 cup mashed ripe bananas (about 3 bananas)
- ½ cup chopped walnuts
- 1 tsp vanilla extract

Instructions:

1. **Prepare the Oven and Pan:**
    1. Preheat your oven to 350°F (175°C). Line a muffin tin with paper liners.
2. **Mix Dry Ingredients:**
    1. In a bowl, whisk together flour, baking powder, baking soda, and salt.
3. **Cream Butter and Sugar:**
    1. In a large bowl, cream together butter and sugar until light and fluffy.
    2. Beat in eggs one at a time, then mix in mashed bananas and vanilla extract.
4. **Combine and Bake:**
    1. Gradually add the dry ingredients to the wet ingredients, mixing until just combined.
    2. Fold in chopped walnuts.
    3. Divide batter evenly among muffin cups.
    4. Bake for 18-22 minutes, or until a toothpick inserted into the center comes out clean.
5. **Cool and Serve:**
    1. Allow muffins to cool in the tin for 5 minutes, then transfer to a wire rack to cool completely.

Banana Almond Smoothie

Ingredients:

- 1 ripe banana
- 1 cup almond milk (or any milk of choice)
- 2 tbsp almond butter
- ½ cup Greek yogurt
- 1 tbsp honey or maple syrup
- 1 cup ice
- A pinch of cinnamon (optional)

Instructions:

1. **Blend Ingredients:**
    1. In a blender, combine banana, almond milk, almond butter, Greek yogurt, honey, and ice.
    2. Blend until smooth.
2. **Serve:**
    1. Pour into glasses and, if desired, sprinkle a pinch of cinnamon on top before serving.

Banana Pecan Pie

Ingredients:

- **For the Crust:**
    - 1 ½ cups all-purpose flour
    - ¼ cup granulated sugar
    - ½ cup unsalted butter, cold and cut into pieces
    - 1 large egg yolk
    - 2-3 tbsp cold water
- **For the Filling:**
    - ¾ cup granulated sugar
    - ½ cup light corn syrup
    - ¼ cup unsalted butter, melted
    - 3 large eggs
    - 1 tsp vanilla extract
    - 1 cup mashed ripe bananas (about 2 bananas)
    - 1 cup chopped pecans

Instructions:

1. **Prepare the Crust:**
    1. In a food processor, combine flour and sugar. Add cold butter and pulse until mixture resembles coarse crumbs.
    2. Add egg yolk and cold water, pulsing until dough comes together.
    3. Press dough into a 9-inch pie pan and chill for 30 minutes.
2. **Prepare the Filling:**
    1. Preheat oven to 350°F (175°C).
    2. In a large bowl, whisk together sugar, corn syrup, melted butter, eggs, and vanilla extract.
    3. Stir in mashed bananas and chopped pecans.
    4. Pour filling into the prepared crust.
3. **Bake:**
    1. Bake for 50-60 minutes, or until filling is set and crust is golden brown.
4. **Cool and Serve:**
    1. Allow pie to cool completely before slicing and serving.

Banana Cinnamon Oatmeal

Ingredients:

- 1 cup rolled oats
- 2 cups milk (dairy or non-dairy)
- 1 ripe banana, sliced
- 1 tbsp maple syrup or honey
- 1 tsp ground cinnamon
- A pinch of salt

Instructions:

1. **Cook Oats:**
    1. In a saucepan, bring milk to a simmer.
    2. Stir in oats and salt. Cook, stirring occasionally, for 5-7 minutes, or until oats are tender.
2. **Add Flavor:**
    1. Stir in sliced banana, maple syrup, and cinnamon.
3. **Serve:**
    1. Serve warm, with additional banana slices and a sprinkle of cinnamon if desired.

Banana Oat Pancakes

Ingredients:

- 1 cup rolled oats
- 1 cup milk (dairy or non-dairy)
- 1 ripe banana, mashed
- 1 large egg
- 1 tsp vanilla extract
- 1 tsp baking powder
- A pinch of salt
- Butter or oil for cooking

Instructions:

1. **Prepare Batter:**
    1. In a blender, combine oats and milk. Blend until smooth.
    2. Add mashed banana, egg, vanilla extract, baking powder, and salt. Blend until well combined.
2. **Cook Pancakes:**
    1. Heat a skillet or griddle over medium heat and lightly grease with butter or oil.
    2. Pour batter onto the skillet to form pancakes. Cook for 2-3 minutes per side, or until golden brown and cooked through.
3. **Serve:**
    1. Serve warm with your favorite toppings.

Banana and Date Energy Balls

Ingredients:

- 1 cup pitted dates
- 1 cup rolled oats
- ½ cup nuts (such as almonds or walnuts)
- 1 ripe banana
- 2 tbsp chia seeds
- 1 tbsp cocoa powder (optional)
- A pinch of salt

Instructions:

1. **Blend Ingredients:**
    1. In a food processor, combine dates, oats, nuts, and a pinch of salt. Process until finely chopped.
    2. Add banana and chia seeds, and cocoa powder if using. Process until mixture comes together.
2. **Form Balls:**
    1. Roll mixture into small balls (about 1 inch in diameter).
3. **Chill:**
    1. Refrigerate for at least 30 minutes before serving.

Banana Cream Bars

Ingredients:

- **For the Crust:**
    - 1 ½ cups graham cracker crumbs
    - ¼ cup granulated sugar
    - 6 tbsp unsalted butter, melted
- **For the Filling:**
    - 1 cup mashed ripe bananas (about 2 bananas)
    - 1 package (8 oz) cream cheese, softened
    - ½ cup powdered sugar
    - 1 cup whipped cream or whipped topping
    - 1 tsp vanilla extract

Instructions:

1. **Prepare the Crust:**
    1. In a bowl, combine graham cracker crumbs, sugar, and melted butter.
    2. Press mixture into the bottom of a greased 9x13-inch baking dish.
2. **Prepare the Filling:**
    1. In a bowl, beat together cream cheese and powdered sugar until smooth.
    2. Mix in mashed bananas and vanilla extract.
    3. Fold in whipped cream or whipped topping until combined.
3. **Assemble and Chill:**
    1. Spread filling over the prepared crust.
    2. Refrigerate for at least 4 hours or until set.
4. **Serve:**
    1. Cut into bars and serve chilled.

Banana Chocolate Chip Cookies

Ingredients:

- 1 cup all-purpose flour
- ½ tsp baking soda
- ¼ tsp salt
- ½ cup unsalted butter, softened
- ¼ cup granulated sugar
- ½ cup packed brown sugar
- 1 large egg
- 1 tsp vanilla extract
- 1 cup mashed ripe bananas (about 2 bananas)
- ½ cup chocolate chips

Instructions:

1. **Prepare the Oven and Pan:**
   1. Preheat your oven to 350°F (175°C). Line a baking sheet with parchment paper.
2. **Mix Dry Ingredients:**
   1. In a bowl, whisk together flour, baking soda, and salt.
3. **Cream Butter and Sugars:**
   1. In a large bowl, cream together butter, granulated sugar, and brown sugar until light and fluffy.
   2. Beat in the egg, vanilla extract, and mashed bananas.
4. **Combine and Bake:**
   1. Gradually add the dry ingredients to the wet ingredients, mixing until just combined.
   2. Fold in chocolate chips.
   3. Drop spoonfuls of dough onto the prepared baking sheet.
   4. Bake for 10-12 minutes, or until edges are golden brown.
5. **Cool and Serve:**
   1. Allow cookies to cool on the baking sheet for a few minutes before transferring to a wire rack to cool completely.

Banana Coconut Energy Balls

Ingredients:

- 1 cup pitted dates
- 1 cup rolled oats
- ½ cup shredded coconut
- 1 ripe banana
- ¼ cup almond butter (or peanut butter)
- 2 tbsp chia seeds
- A pinch of salt

Instructions:

1. **Blend Ingredients:**
   1. In a food processor, combine dates, oats, shredded coconut, and a pinch of salt. Process until finely chopped.
   2. Add banana, almond butter, and chia seeds. Process until the mixture starts to come together.
2. **Form Balls:**
   1. Roll mixture into small balls (about 1 inch in diameter).
3. **Chill:**
   1. Refrigerate for at least 30 minutes before serving.

Banana Raisin Bread

Ingredients:

- 1 ½ cups all-purpose flour
- ½ tsp baking powder
- ½ tsp baking soda
- ¼ tsp salt
- ½ cup unsalted butter, softened
- ½ cup granulated sugar
- ¼ cup brown sugar
- 2 large eggs
- 1 cup mashed ripe bananas (about 2 bananas)
- ½ cup raisins
- 1 tsp vanilla extract
- ½ tsp ground cinnamon (optional)

Instructions:

1. **Prepare the Oven and Pan:**
    1. Preheat your oven to 350°F (175°C). Grease and flour a 9x5-inch loaf pan.
2. **Mix Dry Ingredients:**
    1. In a bowl, whisk together flour, baking powder, baking soda, salt, and cinnamon if using.
3. **Cream Butter and Sugars:**
    1. In a large bowl, cream together butter, granulated sugar, and brown sugar until light and fluffy.
    2. Beat in eggs one at a time, then mix in mashed bananas and vanilla extract.
4. **Combine and Bake:**
    1. Gradually add the dry ingredients to the wet ingredients, mixing until just combined.
    2. Fold in raisins.
    3. Pour batter into the prepared loaf pan.
    4. Bake for 55-60 minutes, or until a toothpick inserted into the center comes out clean.
5. **Cool and Serve:**

1. Allow bread to cool in the pan for 10 minutes, then transfer to a wire rack to cool completely.

Banana Peanut Butter Bars

Ingredients:

- 1 cup rolled oats
- 1 cup mashed ripe bananas (about 2 bananas)
- ½ cup peanut butter
- ¼ cup honey or maple syrup
- ¼ cup mini chocolate chips (optional)
- ¼ cup chopped peanuts (optional)

Instructions:

1. **Prepare the Pan:**
   1. Line an 8x8-inch baking dish with parchment paper.
2. **Mix Ingredients:**
   1. In a bowl, combine oats, mashed bananas, peanut butter, and honey. Mix until well combined.
   2. Stir in chocolate chips and chopped peanuts if using.
3. **Press and Chill:**
   1. Press mixture evenly into the prepared pan.
   2. Refrigerate for at least 2 hours to set.
4. **Cut and Serve:**
   1. Once set, cut into bars and serve.

Banana Caramel Cake

Ingredients:

- **For the Cake:**
    - 1 ½ cups all-purpose flour
    - 1 cup granulated sugar
    - 1 tsp baking powder
    - ½ tsp baking soda
    - ¼ tsp salt
    - ½ cup unsalted butter, softened
    - 2 large eggs
    - 1 cup mashed ripe bananas (about 2 bananas)
    - ½ cup sour cream
    - 1 tsp vanilla extract
- **For the Caramel Sauce:**
    - ½ cup granulated sugar
    - ¼ cup unsalted butter
    - ¼ cup heavy cream
    - 1 tsp vanilla extract

Instructions:

1. **Prepare the Cake:**
    1. Preheat your oven to 350°F (175°C). Grease and flour a 9-inch round cake pan.
2. **Mix Dry Ingredients:**
    1. In a bowl, whisk together flour, sugar, baking powder, baking soda, and salt.
3. **Cream Butter and Sugar:**
    1. In a large bowl, cream together butter and sugar until light and fluffy.
    2. Beat in eggs one at a time, then mix in mashed bananas, sour cream, and vanilla extract.
4. **Combine and Bake:**
    1. Gradually add the dry ingredients to the wet ingredients, mixing until just combined.
    2. Pour batter into the prepared pan.

3. Bake for 30-35 minutes, or until a toothpick inserted into the center comes out clean.

5. **Prepare the Caramel Sauce:**
    1. In a saucepan over medium heat, melt sugar until it turns golden brown.
    2. Stir in butter and continue to cook until melted.
    3. Remove from heat and carefully stir in cream and vanilla extract.
    4. Allow caramel to cool slightly before drizzling over the cooled cake.
6. **Serve:**
    1. Allow cake to cool completely before serving with caramel sauce drizzled on top.

Banana and Yogurt Parfait

Ingredients:

- 2 cups Greek yogurt
- 1 cup granola
- 1 cup sliced ripe bananas
- ¼ cup honey or maple syrup
- Fresh berries for garnish (optional)

Instructions:

1. **Layer Parfait:**
    1. In serving glasses or bowls, layer Greek yogurt, granola, and sliced bananas.
    2. Drizzle with honey or maple syrup.
2. **Garnish and Serve:**
    1. Garnish with fresh berries if desired.
    2. Serve immediately.

Banana Maple Muffins

Ingredients:

- 1 ½ cups all-purpose flour
- ½ cup granulated sugar
- ½ cup maple syrup
- 1 tsp baking powder
- ½ tsp baking soda
- ¼ tsp salt
- ½ cup unsalted butter, melted
- 1 cup mashed ripe bananas (about 2 bananas)
- 1 large egg
- 1 tsp vanilla extract

Instructions:

1. **Prepare the Oven and Pan:**
    1. Preheat your oven to 350°F (175°C). Line a muffin tin with paper liners.
2. **Mix Dry Ingredients:**
    1. In a bowl, whisk together flour, sugar, baking powder, baking soda, and salt.
3. **Combine Wet Ingredients:**
    1. In another bowl, mix melted butter, mashed bananas, maple syrup, egg, and vanilla extract.
4. **Combine and Bake:**
    1. Gradually add the dry ingredients to the wet ingredients, mixing until just combined.
    2. Divide batter evenly among muffin cups.
    3. Bake for 18-22 minutes, or until a toothpick inserted into the center comes out clean.
5. **Cool and Serve:**
    1. Allow muffins to cool in the tin for 5 minutes, then transfer to a wire rack to cool completely.

Banana Crumb Cake

Ingredients:

- **For the Cake:**
    - 1 ½ cups all-purpose flour
    - 1 tsp baking powder
    - ½ tsp baking soda
    - ¼ tsp salt
    - ½ cup unsalted butter, softened
    - ¾ cup granulated sugar
    - 1 large egg
    - 1 cup mashed ripe bananas (about 2 bananas)
    - ½ cup sour cream
    - 1 tsp vanilla extract
- **For the Crumb Topping:**
    - ½ cup all-purpose flour
    - ¼ cup granulated sugar
    - ¼ cup packed brown sugar
    - ¼ cup unsalted butter, cold and cut into pieces
    - ½ tsp ground cinnamon

Instructions:

1. **Prepare the Cake:**
    1. Preheat your oven to 350°F (175°C). Grease and flour an 8-inch square baking pan.
2. **Mix Dry Ingredients:**
    1. In a bowl, whisk together flour, baking powder, baking soda, and salt.
3. **Cream Butter and Sugar:**
    1. In a large bowl, cream together butter and sugar until light and fluffy.
    2. Beat in the egg, then mix in mashed bananas, sour cream, and vanilla extract.
4. **Combine and Bake:**
    1. Gradually add the dry ingredients to the wet ingredients, mixing until just combined.
    2. Pour batter into the prepared pan.
5. **Prepare the Crumb Topping:**

    1. In a bowl, combine flour, granulated sugar, brown sugar, cinnamon, and cold butter.
    2. Use a pastry cutter or fork to mix until crumbly.
6. **Add Topping and Bake:**
    1. Sprinkle crumb topping evenly over the batter.
    2. Bake for 35-40 minutes, or until a toothpick inserted into the center comes out clean.
7. **Cool and Serve:**
    1. Allow cake to cool in the pan for 10 minutes, then transfer to a wire rack to cool completely.

Banana Chocolate Smoothie

Ingredients:

- 1 ripe banana
- 1 cup milk (dairy or non-dairy)
- 2 tbsp cocoa powder
- 2 tbsp honey or maple syrup
- ½ cup Greek yogurt
- 1 cup ice

Instructions:

1. **Blend Ingredients:**
   1. In a blender, combine banana, milk, cocoa powder, honey, Greek yogurt, and ice.
   2. Blend until smooth.
2. **Serve:**
   1. Pour into glasses and serve immediately.

Banana Berry Smoothie

Ingredients:

- 1 ripe banana
- 1 cup mixed berries (fresh or frozen)
- 1 cup milk (dairy or non-dairy)
- ½ cup Greek yogurt
- 1 tbsp honey or maple syrup
- 1 cup ice

Instructions:

1. **Blend Ingredients:**
    1. In a blender, combine banana, mixed berries, milk, Greek yogurt, honey, and ice.
    2. Blend until smooth.
2. **Serve:**
    1. Pour into glasses and serve immediately.

Banana Almond Cake

Ingredients:

- 1 ½ cups all-purpose flour
- 1 cup granulated sugar
- ½ cup almond meal
- 1 tsp baking powder
- ½ tsp baking soda
- ¼ tsp salt
- ½ cup unsalted butter, softened
- 2 large eggs
- 1 cup mashed ripe bananas (about 2 bananas)
- ½ cup sour cream
- 1 tsp vanilla extract
- ¼ cup sliced almonds (for topping)

Instructions:

1. **Prepare the Oven and Pan:**
    1. Preheat your oven to 350°F (175°C). Grease and flour an 8-inch round cake pan.
2. **Mix Dry Ingredients:**
    1. In a bowl, whisk together flour, sugar, almond meal, baking powder, baking soda, and salt.
3. **Cream Butter and Sugar:**
    1. In a large bowl, cream together butter and sugar until light and fluffy.
    2. Beat in eggs one at a time, then mix in mashed bananas, sour cream, and vanilla extract.
4. **Combine and Bake:**
    1. Gradually add the dry ingredients to the wet ingredients, mixing until just combined.
    2. Pour batter into the prepared pan.
    3. Sprinkle sliced almonds on top.
    4. Bake for 30-35 minutes, or until a toothpick inserted into the center comes out clean.
5. **Cool and Serve:**

1. Allow cake to cool in the pan for 10 minutes, then transfer to a wire rack to cool completely.

Banana Nut Cupcakes

Ingredients:

- 1 ¼ cups all-purpose flour
- ½ cup granulated sugar
- ¼ cup packed brown sugar
- 1 tsp baking powder
- ½ tsp baking soda
- ¼ tsp salt
- ½ cup unsalted butter, softened
- 2 large eggs
- 1 cup mashed ripe bananas (about 2 bananas)
- ½ cup chopped nuts (such as walnuts or pecans)
- 1 tsp vanilla extract

Instructions:

1. **Prepare the Oven and Pan:**
    1. Preheat your oven to 350°F (175°C). Line a muffin tin with paper liners.
2. **Mix Dry Ingredients:**
    1. In a bowl, whisk together flour, granulated sugar, brown sugar, baking powder, baking soda, and salt.
3. **Cream Butter and Sugars:**
    1. In a large bowl, cream together butter, granulated sugar, and brown sugar until light and fluffy.
    2. Beat in eggs one at a time, then mix in mashed bananas and vanilla extract.
4. **Combine and Bake:**
    1. Gradually add the dry ingredients to the wet ingredients, mixing until just combined.
    2. Fold in chopped nuts.
    3. Divide batter evenly among muffin cups.
    4. Bake for 18-22 minutes, or until a toothpick inserted into the center comes out clean.
5. **Cool and Serve:**
    1. Allow cupcakes to cool in the tin for 5 minutes, then transfer to a wire rack to cool completely.

Banana Pineapple Smoothie

Ingredients:

- 1 ripe banana
- 1 cup pineapple chunks (fresh or frozen)
- 1 cup coconut milk (or any milk of choice)
- ½ cup Greek yogurt
- 1 tbsp honey or maple syrup
- 1 cup ice

Instructions:

1. **Blend Ingredients:**
    1. In a blender, combine banana, pineapple chunks, coconut milk, Greek yogurt, honey, and ice.
    2. Blend until smooth.
2. **Serve:**
    1. Pour into glasses and serve immediately.

Banana and Nut Granola

Ingredients:

- 2 cups old-fashioned rolled oats
- ½ cup chopped nuts (such as almonds, walnuts, or pecans)
- ¼ cup honey or maple syrup
- ¼ cup coconut oil, melted
- 1 ripe banana, mashed
- ¼ cup dried fruit (such as raisins or cranberries)
- 1 tsp vanilla extract
- A pinch of salt

Instructions:

1. **Prepare the Oven:**
    1. Preheat your oven to 350°F (175°C). Line a baking sheet with parchment paper.
2. **Mix Ingredients:**
    1. In a large bowl, combine oats, chopped nuts, and salt.
    2. In a separate bowl, mix together honey, melted coconut oil, mashed banana, and vanilla extract.
    3. Pour wet ingredients over dry ingredients and mix until evenly coated.
3. **Bake:**
    1. Spread granola mixture evenly on the prepared baking sheet.
    2. Bake for 20-25 minutes, stirring halfway through, until golden brown.
4. **Cool and Store:**
    1. Allow granola to cool completely before stirring in dried fruit.
    2. Store in an airtight container.

Banana Cheesecake Bars

Ingredients:

- **For the Crust:**
    - 1 ½ cups graham cracker crumbs
    - ¼ cup granulated sugar
    - 6 tbsp unsalted butter, melted
- **For the Filling:**
    - 1 package (8 oz) cream cheese, softened
    - ½ cup granulated sugar
    - 2 large eggs
    - 1 cup mashed ripe bananas (about 2 bananas)
    - 1 tsp vanilla extract
    - ¼ cup sour cream

Instructions:

1. **Prepare the Crust:**
    1. Preheat your oven to 325°F (160°C). Grease an 8x8-inch baking pan.
2. **Mix Crust Ingredients:**
    1. In a bowl, combine graham cracker crumbs, sugar, and melted butter.
    2. Press mixture into the bottom of the prepared pan.
3. **Prepare the Filling:**
    1. In a large bowl, beat together cream cheese and sugar until smooth.
    2. Beat in eggs one at a time.
    3. Mix in mashed bananas, vanilla extract, and sour cream until well combined.
4. **Bake:**
    1. Pour filling over the crust.
    2. Bake for 35-40 minutes, or until the center is set.
5. **Cool and Serve:**
    1. Allow bars to cool to room temperature, then refrigerate for at least 4 hours before cutting into squares and serving.

Banana Pudding Trifle

Ingredients:

- 1 package (3.4 oz) vanilla pudding mix
- 2 cups milk
- 1 cup heavy cream
- 2 tbsp powdered sugar
- 3 ripe bananas, sliced
- 1 package (8 oz) vanilla wafers
- ¼ cup chopped nuts (optional, for garnish)

Instructions:

1. **Prepare Pudding:**
    1. In a bowl, whisk together pudding mix and milk until thickened.
2. **Prepare Whipped Cream:**
    1. In a separate bowl, whip heavy cream and powdered sugar until stiff peaks form.
3. **Assemble Trifle:**
    1. In a trifle dish or large bowl, layer vanilla wafers, pudding, and banana slices.
    2. Top with a layer of whipped cream.
4. **Chill:**
    1. Refrigerate for at least 2 hours before serving.
5. **Garnish and Serve:**
    1. Garnish with chopped nuts if desired before serving.

www.ingramcontent.com/pod-product-compliance
Lightning Source LLC
LaVergne TN
LVHW081320060526
838201LV00055B/2385